FROM MEDIA SHY TO MEDIA SAVVY

14 simple strategies
to nail your next media interview

AMANDA MILLS

FROM MEDIA SHY TO MEDIA SAVVY

14 simple strategies
to nail your next media interview

AMANDA MILLS

Copyright © 2024 Amanda Mills
Amanda Mills Author & Consultant

All rights reserved. This book or any portion thereof may not be reproduced or used in any manner whatsoever without the express written permission of the author except for the use of brief quotations in articles or reviews.

ISBN PAPERBACK: 978-1-7636316-1-8

ISBN HARDBACK: 978-1-7636316-0-1

ISBN EBOOK: 978-1-7636316-2-5

Book Cover, Typesetting and Layout Design Copyright © 2024 Maja Creative

Art Direction by Maja Wolnik of Maja Creative

Graphic Design by Monika Majewska of Maja Creative

DEDICATION

The book is dedicated to my son Regent Mills and the wonderful conversations we share.

It also dedicated to anyone struggling with the confidence to shine their light brighter and share their words of wisdom to the world. You never know who your expertise with help until you share your knowledge..

TABLE OF CONTENTS

01 INTRODUCTION 9

02 6 KEY TRAITS OF A SUCCESSFUL COMMUNICATOR 13

03 SOME HELPFUL MEDIA TIPS 17

04 9 TIPS FOR A SUCCESSFUL INTERVIEW 21

05 MEDIA GROUND RULES 25

06 THE RIGHT WAY TO TELL REPORTERS ABOUT YOURSELF 31

07 THE INTERVIEW: THE 3 QUESTIONS REPORTERS ALWAYS ASK 35

08 5 WAYS TO AVOID BEING MISQUOTED BY REPORTERS 39

09 9 TIPS FOR BETTER RADIO/PODCAST INTERVIEWS 45

10 10 TIPS FOR A SUCCESSFUL TELEVISION INTERVIEW 51

11 BODY LANGUAGE 57

12 SOCIAL MEDIA MODERATION 63

13 MANAGING ANXIETY 67

14 PRACTICAL EXERCISES 71

15 PRACTICAL PRE-INTERVIEW TIPS 75

16 MY OFFER TO YOU 79

17 ABOUT THE AUTHOR 81

CHAPTER 01

INTRODUCTION

WE LIVE IN A
MEDIA-DOMINATED
SOCIETY

INTRODUCTION TO MEDIA SHY TO MEDIA SAVVY

We live in a media-dominated society where anyone and everyone can be called upon to make a statement or provide their expert opinion to media. The effects of interviews can be long lasting, as a digital presence can be searched for and found many years later.

Through media training, essential skills for learning to engage with the media are built. *Media Shy to Media Savvy* provides 14 media training strategies so you can confidently nail your next media interview.

WHY YOU NEED MEDIA TRAINING

- To feel confident, concise and clear when answering questions.
- To help get across key messages and a call to action.
- To avoid embarrassment and potential negative outcomes, both for yourself and your organisation.
- To learn how to engage with your identified audiences through different media channels.
- To feel prepared for an upcoming media opportunity at short notice.

CHAPTER 02

6 KEY TRAITS
OF A SUCCESSFUL
COMMUNICATOR

ANY FORM OF MEDIA ENGAGEMENT IS DIRECTED AT YOUR AUDIENCE

6 KEY TRAITS OF A SUCCESSFUL COMMUNICATOR

To successfully captivate youraudience and gain credibility, there are six key communication traits you should aim to improve. These are:

01 **Authenticity** – what you say, you believe and is based on facts and your work history as an expert.

02 **Confidence** – you are at ease speaking to the media and enjoy the opportunity.

03 **Flexibility** – you can adapt to the situation at hand and answer unexpected questions confidently.

04 **You understand your audience** – any form of media engagement is directed at your audience. The media is merely a channel for talking to your audience; thus, you want to engage the audience, not just the interviewer.

05 **Be concise** – you say things in a short, concise manner. Being 'long-winded' only confuses and loses your audience.

06 **Be engaging** – you are expressive and knowledgeable. Use descriptive examples where possible.

CHAPTER 03

SOME HELPFUL MEDIA TIPS

THE FUNDAMENTALS ALWAYS COME DOWN TO PREPARATION

SOME HELPFUL MEDIA TIPS

BE PREPARED, NEVER WING IT

The first lesson is not to wing it. Just because you're immersed in a subject every day doesn't mean you can spontaneously pull on the right threads to weave together a public performance, especially if there is a camera or microphone pointed at you.

The fundamentals always come down to preparation. Whether you work with a professional media coach or prefer to go it alone, invest time and effort in rehearsals. Get your spouse, work colleague or a trusted friend to lob questions at you. Make sure those lobs have some zing. How will you respond to tough or hostile questions? Do you have a clear, honest and appropriate answer to the most negative query you can imagine?

Plan your answers with key messages and try to second-guess supplementary questions.

Make sure to research your listeners and their expectations beforehand. In any interview, you're really speaking via the reporter to their readers, listeners or viewers. Videotape your performance and use the results to make changes.

Sometimes you cannot see what others see, so by recording and watching back, you can view yourself from the perspective of your audience and will notice aspects you may never have noticed before.

Try being interviewed by local media and/or over the phone a few times before accepting live radio and television interviews. Present at friendly networking events or meetings to practice presentation skills. Gauge what content your live audience is particularly drawn to.

DEVELOP YOUR KEY MESSAGE AND FIND WAYS TO COMMUNICATE IT

The real difference between talking to the media and talking directly to an audience, of course, comes down to control. For a speech, you pick and choose your points and timing. But for interviews, reporters have control and can often lead the interview in unexpected directions.

That doesn't mean you lean back and remain passive. The idea is to subtly present your key messages while still responding to questions. At the outset, it helps if you have a call to action or a link ready where the reporter or audience can find out more information such as a website link, landing page or social media handle.

Once you've accomplished that, continue reading our nine tips for a successful interview to help you master the art of getting out your preferred message.

CHAPTER 04

9 TIPS FOR A SUCCESSFUL INTERVIEW

SET GOALS FOR EVERY APPEARANCE. ONE TOOL IS 'OSTA': OBJECTIVE, STRATEGY, TACTICS AND AUDIENCE.

9 TIPS FOR A SUCCESSFUL INTERVIEW

01 **Set goals for every appearance.** One tool is 'OSTA': objective, strategy, tactics and audience. Everything communicated should have an OSTA plan. Plan to hammer home your key messages. For interviews, keep answers to about 25 to 40 seconds each — especially for TV or radio.

02 **Nothing is 100% off the record.** Once notes are made, reporters, editors and producers can review them. This goes for all appearances, not just interviews. Whatever you say — anywhere — can follow you around endlessly and perhaps disastrously. If you don't know the answer to a question, say so. Then later, be certain to get back to the reporter with an answer.

03 **Watch your body language.** Even in positive interview situations, interviewees sometimes look tense or stiff, which can have a big impact on your credibility. Before on-camera interviews, if there is time, do some exercises or walk around to relax your body.

04 **Use simple language.** Every industry has its own jargon, particularly the medical industry. Make sure you use a language your audience can clearly understand. Use an everyday example to get your point across. Include compelling statistics and facts.

05 **Learn how to "bridge".** This technique allows you to deflect any attempts to derail your message. "Bridging" creates a transition so that you can move from one subject to the message you want to communicate.

First answer the direct question, then transition to your message. For example:
- "Before we get off that topic, let me just add..."
- "Let me put that in perspective..."
- "It's important to remember that..."

06 **Create a grab for media.** A grab is one of the most important parts of a broadcast media interview. It grabs attention and may include your brand name. An example grab I used with a client was "less Screen time more Green time". This was used to demonstrate the importance of regular eye check-ups by discussing the topical subject of too much screen time.

07 **Prepare your own Q&A ahead of time.** Ask the reporter, producer or podcast host for questions ahead of time so you can prepare your answers. If they can't provide questions ahead of the interview, then put together a list of the questions you are most likely going to be asked. You could even send these Q&As to the reporter or producer, who may decide to ask some of the questions.

08 **Prepare key takeaways.** Always plan the points or facts you want the reporter and, by extension, the audience to walk away thinking about. Narrow the focus, then to get listeners to remember you, deliver those points passionately and succinctly through analogies and describing experiences or case studies.

09 **Finally, it's not over when it's over.** Make sure to track the results and get reviews of your performance. Ask friends and peers how well your message went over. Make tweaks and improvements based on constructive feedback.

CHAPTER 05

MEDIA
GROUND
RULES

NEVER SAY ANYTHING OFF THE RECORD

MEDIA GROUND RULES

NEVER SAY ANYTHING OFF THE RECORD

It is a blurred term for many reporters, as each has a differing definition. The best way to approach an interview is to assume that everything you say will be used in the broadcast or publication. Thus, choose your words accordingly.

8 QUESTIONS TO ASK BEFORE EVERY INTERVIEW

Do not conduct an interview the moment the reporter calls. Instead, offer to return their call promptly and take at least a few minutes to prepare for the interview before you speak.

Before you hang up from that initial phone call, take a few minutes to "interview" the reporter. Many journalists are willing to share the basics about the stories they're working on and any insight they offer will help you better prepare. Below are eight questions to consider asking reporters. Don't ask all of these for every interview, as journalists don't appreciate being grilled. They'll offer some of this information on their own anyway, so just fill in any gaps by asking the most relevant of these questions:

01 **"Who are you?"** No, you shouldn't ask that question verbatim, but collect the basics – their name, the name of the news organisation for which they work and their job title(e.g., news reporter, health reporter, lifestyle reporter etc).

02 **"Can you tell me about the story you're working on?"** Keep this question open-ended and remain quiet while the reporter speaks (the more they say, the more you'll learn). Feel free to ask follow-up questions and to clarify any points you don't fully understand. Ask the journalist or producer to email you an example of a similar story or interview.

03 **"Are you approaching this story from any perspective?"** Some reporters will bristle if you ask, "What's your angle?". This question aims to elicit the same information in a subtle manner.

04 **"Who else are you interviewing?"** Reporters may play it close to their chest on this one but it's worth asking. You'll be able to get a sense of the story's tone by learning whether the other sources in the story are friendly or antagonistic toward your cause.

05 **"What's the format?"** For print and digital interviews, this question will help you determine whether reporters just need a quick quote from you or whether they're writing an in-depth piece that will focus extensively on the topic. For broadcast interviews, you'll be able to learn whether the interview will be live, live-to-tape or edited. For television, you may also want to ask if the format will be on location, on-set or in a different studio.

06 **"What do you need from me?"** Ask the reporter how much time the interview will last and where the reporter wants to conduct the interview. Also, ask if you can provide any press releases, fact sheets, photos, videos or other supplementary documents. You can often expand your presence in a story — and influence the narrative — if the reporter chooses to use your supporting materials.

07 **"Who will be doing the interview?"** For most radio, television and podcast interviews, you will be contacted initially by an off-air producer rather than by an on-air personality. Ask for the name of the person conducting the interview.

08 **"When are you publishing or airing the story?"** Find out when it will be published or airing. Review the story as soon as it comes out. If it's a positive story, share it both online and in regular newsletters. If it's a negative story or factually incorrect, consider issuing a response or contacting the reporter or editor to discuss the coverage.

One final note: Before an interview, tell reporters how you prefer to be named or identified. Include your title and company name and spell your full name. Nothing is worse than seeing your name or company's name mangled in front of millions of viewers!

CHAPTER 06

THE RIGHT WAY TO TELL REPORTERS ABOUT YOURSELF

THE FIRST QUESTION YOU ARE ASKED IS ALMOST ALWAYS THE SAME

THE RIGHT WAY TO TELL REPORTERS ABOUT YOURSELF

THE FIRST QUESTION YOU ARE ASKED IS ALMOST ALWAYS THE SAME:

Can you tell me about your business/company?

Nine times out of a 10, the spokesperson will say something like:

"Well, the Association of Optometrists is a non-profit organisation with 30 employees working in four state-wide offices to promote accredited optometrists."

DID THIS STATEMENT GRAB YOU?

There's a better way. When a reporter asks you a wide-open question, such as "What do you do?", begin with the "why" – the interesting context that makes your "what" more evocative. Imagine if the spokesperson above had responded this way:

"The *Association of Optometrists is a non-profit organisation that provide practical advice and tips on how to care for your family's eyesight.*"

Starting with the "why" does that – and it allows you to explain who you are in a way the audience will understand immediately.

Next time you're asked an open-ended question, ditch the bland organisational mission statement and remember to **start with the "why".**

CHAPTER 07

THE INTERVIEW: THE 3 QUESTIONS REPORTERS ALWAYS ASK

THE MEDIA WILL IDENTIFY YOU AS A REPRESENTATIVE OF YOUR ORGANISATION

THE INTERVIEW: THE 3 QUESTIONS REPORTERS ALWAYS ASK

1. QUESTIONS YOU DON'T KNOW THE ANSWER TO

Many people get stumped during a live interview when they're asked a question to which they can't give you the answer.

For example, a doctor may be asked, "Does standing cause varicose veins?". If they can't provide a factual answer based on scientific evidence and within medical guidelines, they might stumble before finally saying, "I can't confirm this.".

Here's a better way to handle that question during friendly interviews: *"Varicose veins usually run in families. If one parent has varicose veins, you have about a 33 per cent chance of developing vein problems; if it's both parents, this increases to about 90 per cent.*

Sitting and standing for prolonged periods can pose problems to leg health."

2. QUESTIONS THAT CALL FOR SPECULATION

If asked a question that calls for speculation or there isn't scientific evidence, you will need to stick to facts and evidence no matter how many times you are asked the same question.

Here's a question on the topic of eye damage due to excessive use of digital devices: *"Are you seeing an increase in cases of eye damage in children due to use of digital devices?"*

The following answer below sticks to the scientific evidence but still includes a key message regarding the importance of eye checks for children.

"Finding up-to-date numbers on how many children suffer from eye issues is extremely hard as studies into the area are limited. We do know that one in four children have an undetected eye problem. It's important to have your child's eye checked regularly by a qualified optometrist."

If pressed again, you can follow up with, *"Well, although I can't speculate, I can tell you that..."*. Stick to the evidence but emphasise your key message here.

3. QUESTIONS THAT ASK FOR YOUR PERSONAL OPINION

When you are identified as a spokesperson for your own company, group or organisation, there's no such thing as a personal opinion.

The media will identify you as a representative of your organisation. Period.

Therefore, do not offer a personal opinion. Instead, say, *"Well, I'm speaking for the organisation, not myself, and what we can indicate is..."*

CHAPTER 08

5 WAYS TO AVOID BEING MISQUOTED BY REPORTERS

YOU HAVE A LOT MORE CONTROL THAN YOU THINK

5 WAYS TO AVOID BEING MISQUOTED BY REPORTERS

There's good news and bad news for spokespeople who have suffered an infuriating misquote. The bad news is that you can never guarantee that a reporter will quote you correctly. But the good news is that you have a lot more control than you think – and you can dramatically increase the odds that the reporter will get your story right by using the five techniques below:

01 **Give Them the Facts:** The more you say, the more you stray. A lot of spokespeople get misquoted because they say too much. Instead of spending most of your interviews providing reporters with endless background, write a one-page or two-page fact sheet, which lays out the basic facts and statistics on the topic. Consider providing reporters this written fact sheet in advance of your interview. By doing so, your quote will contain your interpretation of the facts instead of raw facts devoid of context. Because you've said less and repeatedly emphasised the meaning of the story, you've given reporters more opportunities not only to get your quote right but to make it meaningful.

02 **Listen for Clues:** If you're giving a phone interview, listen for the sound of typing on the other end – you'll hear it when you say something that intrigues the reporter. That's your cue to slow down, make sure the reporter has time to capture every word and repeat what you've just said. The same is true during an in-person interview when a reporter is scribbling notes in a notepad. When you see a reporter scribbling notes, slow down and repeat your point.

03 **Suggest Answering by Email:** Some reporters allow interviewees to respond to questions over email, which allows you to retain total control of your words. Just be sure to have a colleague or publicist check your responses for unintended meanings and phrases that can be taken out of context. Find out the word limit and keep responses short and concise.

04 **Now, What Did I Just Say?** Although reporters are under no obligation to read your quotes back to you, many of them will. If you don't like the way you said something, they may not change it – but if you said something factually inaccurate, they usually will. You should ask them to read back your quotes during the interview, not afterwards. You can also offer to help the reporter fact check the finished story. If you don't like the way the journalist framed the story, they probably won't change it – but they will correct a "fact" that's inaccurate.

05 **Ask for Questions Prior to an Interview:** Some journalists/producers will send you the questions so you can prepare for the interview. You can let the journalist know in advance if you are unable to answer any of these questions. Having the questions will give you further insight into the story angle and if you feel uncomfortable you will have the opportunity to either decline the interview or thoughtfully prepare your answers, so you aren't misquoted.

CHAPTER 09

9 TIPS FOR BETTER RADIO/PODCAST INTERVIEWS

FIND DIFFERENT WAYS OF ARTICULATING THE MAIN POINTS

9 TIPS FOR BETTER RADIO/PODCAST INTERVIEWS

01 **Radio Interviews Can Begin Abruptly.** Most radio stations arrange to call you rather than having you call into the studio (it can work either way but many producers prefer to control the timing by calling the interviewee themselves). Most producers will call before the interview begins, allowing you to listen for a few minutes and get a feel for the program's tone. But other producers wait for the last possible second, meaning you're on the air within seconds of picking up the phone. When you pick up the phone, be ready to go live at a second's notice – or on no notice at all.

02 **Help Your Host.** Short answers allow the host to ask another question, take another phone call or throw to commercial – so keep your answers to 30 seconds or less. Finish your answer with a declarative sentence that ends on a vocal downtick to make it clear to the host that you've completed your answer.

03 **Express Passion**. Sure, you're on the radio. But listeners will "hear it" if you stand, use well-timed gestures and smile – so get a telephone headset and gesture away. Try to match or slightly exceed the host's energy level to avoid sounding flat.

04 **Don't Depend On Them To Make The Plug.** During some radio interviews the host gives the wrong plug. Another host may offer no plug at all. Although most experienced hosts are adept at sending their listeners to your website or social media, some aren't. That means it's up to you to mention that information a couple of times throughout the interview. You can help the host's odds of getting the plug right by sending the information you'd like plugged in advance of the interview. I would send the producer a shortened version of your bio in advance, which many hosts use verbatim on the air.

05 **High Drop-in, Drop-Out Rates.** Many people who are listening at the beginning of your segment aren't going to be there at the end. Other listeners will join in the middle. Therefore, repeat your main messages – or themes – numerous times during the interview. You shouldn't use the same words, so find different ways of articulating the main points.

06 **Treat Long-winded Live Callers With Respect**. If you do live radio interviews long enough, you'll get the long-winded caller who goes on an angry rant that has little to do with your interview topic. Maintain the high ground. The public recognises angry callers for what they are, so impress the audience with your graceful and kind handling of the caller. That doesn't mean you can't push back on incorrect assertions respectfully. It offers an opportunity to educate the public about the subject matter and to demonstrate your expertise.

07 **Radio Hosts Hang Up On You**. At the end of most radio interviews, the host hangs up the phone. They're not being rude – they must move on to the next segment and clear the studio line for the next guest. Still, it's recommended you stay on the line when the interview ends. Some hosts (or producers) will pick up the phone to thank you, while some will even ask your availability for a future interview.

08 **Make Sure You Have Clear Mobile Phone Reception and Strong Wi-Fi for Zoom**. Some radio interviews will be in-studio however some are by your mobile phone so make sure you choose a location that has strong mobile reception. Likewise, podcasts are often done via Zoom or another online platform so make sure you have strong Wi-Fi on the day of your interview. Also make sure you choose a quiet location without barking dogs and family interruptions. Think about your location ahead of time.

09 **Create A Professional Background for Zoom Interviews**. Since COVID, we have seen an increase in interviews taking place via Zoom to your location. In many cases, this may be when you're at home. Make sure you create a professional on-brand background for your interview. You may have books you have written strategically placed in the background. Create a miniset with plants or a bookcase behind you. Make sure you don't have family members, pets or work colleagues walking by and interrupting the interview. Not only is this unprofessional it could also take you off track.

CHAPTER 10

10 TIPS FOR A SUCCESSFUL TELEVISION INTERVIEW

TAKE CONTROL OF YOUR ENVIRONMENT AND ASK FOR ANY CHANGES AHEAD OF THE INTERVIEW

10 TIPS FOR A SUCCESSFUL TELEVISION INTERVIEW

01 **Arrive early:** Avoid unnecessary stress by allowing plenty of extra time. That buffer will be valuable if the producer, makeup artist or crew is running behind when you arrive.

02 **Bring makeup:** Most major networks and some larger local stations provide a makeup artist. Ask in advance whether you will have access to one but bring your own makeup and hair products either way, just to be safe.

03 **Look in the mirror:** Do a final check in the mirror before your interview begins. Make sure you don't have lipstick smeared on your teeth or big chunks of food stuck in-between teeth.

04 **Check your microphone and test your earpiece:** You will often wear a lapel microphone during your interview. The wires should be hidden, so you can run the cord beneath your top or tape the cord to the back of your tie. Make sure the microphone isn't brushing up against clothing or jewellery, which will make you sound muffled.

05 **Turn off your mobile phone:** Little is more distracting than a mobile phone ringing in middle of an interview. Also, the phone's signal can interfere with the audio. Vibrate mode isn't good enough - power your phone completely off.

06 **Turn the monitor off:** Television monitors in the studio often show a feed that is delayed by a fraction of a second. Television monitors can be extremely distracting, so ask the crew to turn off any monitors or to turn them away. If you are filmed live from another studio, make sure you are looking straight down the camera. Take control of your environment and ask for any changes ahead of the interview.

07 **Beware of the split screen:** In some formats, you will appear on camera even when you're not speaking. Those "split screen" shots show you and at least one other person at the same time. "Reaction" shots will show your reaction to another guest's comments. Act as if you're always on, being careful not to wipe your face, adjust your hair or fix your outfit during your segment.

08 **Restrict your nodding:** It's normal to nod when listening to someone else but nodding can send the wrong message if you disagree with the premise of someone's question or comment. Listen attentively but only nod along if you agree.

09 **Avoid (or pre-plan) props:** We've all seen that television guest who holds up a piece of paper or newspaper article during a television appearance. Few people know how to position an item properly for the camera, so it usually ends up distracting the

audience. If you want to show something during your interview, talk to the producer first. The producer can help the crew prepare for the shot in advance.

10. **Stay in your seat:** Avoid the temptation to flee your chair the moment your segment ends. Maintain your pose for a few seconds, remaining seated until a member of the crew tells you you're clear. This same applies to a live cross on location.

CHAPTER 11

BODY
LANGUAGE

GIVE YOURSELF A MOMENT TO STRUCTURE YOUR ANSWER BY PAUSING BEFORE YOU DELIVER IT

BODY LANGUAGE

EYE CONTACT

A media spokesperson who maintains eye contact just 40 – 60 percent of the time will fail. On television, the lack of eye contact comes across as nervousness (at best) or evasiveness and defensiveness (at worst). Darting eyes can make you appear nervous or insincere.

In general, television guests will look to one of two places, depending on the format: at the interviewer or at the camera. Regardless of the format, you should lock your eyes at the interviewer or camera and never let go. Aim for 100% eye contact.

Keeping your eyes locked in a fixed position during an entire interview will probably not feel natural, at least at first. That's because we often look away when trying to retrieve information from our brain (depending on the type of information, we either look up, to the side or down).

But since great spokespeople do most of their thinking before the interview begins, there's no need for them to look anywhere but at their target.

Finally, a word about straight-to-camera interviews, in which interviewees must stare at the lens or, for a remote interview via Zoom, the camera on your computer. It's a tough format. Try practising by delivering your answers to a specific place on your office wall or even by drawing a face on a sheet of paper and taping it just below the lens. Whatever it takes, lock your eyes and don't let go. Treat the camera lens as a person.

GESTURES

Using hand gestures grabs attention, increases the impact of communication and helps individuals retain more of the information they are hearing!

When you incorporate gestures into your delivery, your words get better. The physical act of gesturing helps you form clearer thoughts and speak in tight, staccato sentences.

For seated interviews, keep your arms open and ready to gesture at any moment. When not gesturing, keep your arms on your lap with your hands near your knees. Avoid clasping your hands, which is regarded as a "closed" form of communication. For standing interviews, keep your arms by your side or, even better, in front of your torso. Avoid hugging your body in any way and resist the temptation to place your hands in your pockets.

POSTURE

Try this exercise to perfect your posture:

- Slump back into your chair for a moment.
- Comfortable? Good. Now try to gesture with genuine enthusiasm.
- If you're like most people, it wasn't easy. The gestures probably felt a bit forced and were almost certainly too casual for a media interview.
- Okay, now lean forward in your chair. Plant your feet firmly on the floor in front of you and try to gesture again.
- It probably felt better, right?
- More natural, more authentic, and less forced?

Leaning forward and projecting energy outward may seem obvious but many people begin their first interview by slumping into their chair. Doing so inevitably dampens their energy and decreases their volume – worse, the passive position often makes them a little slower on their feet.

For standing interviews, try placing one foot slightly in front of the other. Doing so prevents the dreaded side-to-side sway and helps keep your energy aimed forward.

For seated interviews, move forward so you're only sitting on the front half of the chair.

Lean forward a bit to help increase your energy and ensure that the camera's main focus is on your face, not your body.

VOICE

Eliminate the Umms and Ahhs. It's important to note that almost everyone uses some verbal filler in their speech – and that's okay. It only becomes a problem when it distracts an audience. So don't judge yourself on a scale of perfection. If you utter a few "umms," you're fine. If they litter your speech, try the two techniques listed below.

The first technique deals with verbal filler that occurs at the beginning of an answer. That "articulated pause" is understandable since you likely haven't formed your complete thought yet.

Instead of speaking immediately, give yourself a moment to structure your answer by pausing before you deliver it. A short pause is less distracting to an audience than an articulated pause.

It's even easier if the interview isn't live. The audience will rarely see your pauses in an edited interview, so take your time before answering a question – even if that means you pause for 10 or 15 seconds. That tactic not only helps eliminate verbal filler but allows you to think of a better answer that concisely articulates your main message.

If the interview is live, you obviously can't pause for quite as long – but taking a one-second beat to think is okay (the audience is often accustomed to a delay anyway, so they often won't know the difference). Just be careful if you're entering a hostile interview, where the pauses can be edited against you.

CHAPTER 12

SOCIAL MEDIA
MODERATION

ALWAYS BE MINDFUL OF YOUR ONLINE PRESENCE

SOCIAL MEDIA MODERATION

Before any form of media engagement, it is best to conduct a thorough evaluation of your social media presence. You will be googled and searched, by both the journalist/reporter and your audience, thus, it is wise to be mindful about what you put online. Any controversial comments or inappropriate photos may be used against you and the organisation you represent.

THE SOCIAL MEDIA CHECK:

On Facebook, have you activated your settings to private? Or, if you have a public profile, have you taken down photos that you do not want to share with a large public? Have you taken down comments that you wouldn't like people to associate with you?

Ask yourself the same questions for your Twitter/X, LinkedIn, Instagram, Google Plus and TikTok accounts.

Social media is the way you present yourself to the world and is an avenue for investigation for both journalists and potential employees. In fact, many TV producers and reporters source stories from Instagram and TikTok.

Remember: always be mindful of your online presence.

CHAPTER 13

MANAGING ANXIETY

REMEMBER THAT IT IS COMPLETELY NATURAL TO FEEL SOME LEVEL OF ANXIETY

MANAGING ANXIETY

Many people become anxious in an interview situation, whether that is with media or a job interview.

It is important to remember that it is completely natural to feel some level of anxiety and it can help in your overall performance.

HERE ARE SOME TIPS TO HELP MANAGE YOUR ANXIETY:

- Concentrate on the task at hand. This will stop you from focusing on potential anxiety.
- Control your environment. If you're at ease in your environment, you'll feel less stress and anxiety.
- Don't judge yourself for being anxious.be aware that 'yes I have anxiety'but there is nothing wrong with that.
- Shift your focus from yourself to the interviewer by focusing on someone else.
- You'll be less self-conscious and this will help ease the anxiety levels.

CHAPTER 14

PRACTICAL EXERCISES

CONNECT WITH YOUR BREATH

PRACTICAL EXERCISES

VOCAL WARMUPS

- Connect with your breath.
- Warm up your mouth with vocal warmups repeating these words: "Red leather, Yellow leather" or "Unique, New York".

RELEASING TENSION

- Perform a 5-minute relaxation exercise or breathing exercise.
- Remain still and present.

CHAPTER 15

PRACTICAL PRE-INTERVIEW TIPS

ALLOW YOUR PERSONALITY TO SHOW THROUGH AND BE YOUR AUTHENTIC SELF

PRACTICAL PRE-INTERVIEW TIPS

01 **Avoid caffeine** – caffeine leads to dehydration which combine with anxiety, will lead to symptoms such as dry mouth. It also over stimulates an in a heightened state of anxiety you need to be calm and composed.

02 **Hydration** – a symptom of anxiety is a dry mouth, so it is very important to keep hydrated. Have some water on hand at all times and feel comfortable to drink it as required.

03 **Food** – to keep your energy levels up, healthy low gi foods are best for a sustained release of encrgy.

04 **Dress for the environment** – be sure to ask when and where the interview is to be held. If it outdoors, then make sure to dress for the weather. The more comfortable you feel, the better you will come across.

05 **Clothing and appearance** – it's important to understand how your appearance affects your image an how you're perceived. A suit and tie presents a corporate, sensible image, while jeans and t-shirt relay a more laid back casual persona. When it comes to dressing, it's best to avoid patterns and overly loud clothing. Wearing light tonal colours, such as blue always looks good on camera. With

make-up, it's best to keep it natural and simplistic. Avoid tight clothing and check how the outfit will look when sitting as opposed to standing. Is your shirt too tight? Are buttons undone? Make sure a dress hemline is long enough for seated interviews.

06 **Be yourself** – allow your personality to show through and be your authentic self. Anyone listening or watching your interview will have more trust in what you're saying if they feel you have some emotional connection to your message and are speaking from the heart.

MY OFFER TO YOU

Now that you learnt valuable skills in preparation for your next interview with media, why not take your professional skills to the next level by booking an online or onsite media training workshop.

The media training workshop can be conducted with up to four individuals either online or in person and will help you identify the areas you and your colleagues need to level up prior to your next interview with media.

We start with a list of tailored questions that are specific to your industry that media will most likely ask and help you deliver your responses in an authentic, confident and media savvy manner.

We mimic a real-life interview scenario so you can practice your interview techniques and refine your interview style and answers. We deep dive into how to take control of the interview environment so you feel at ease.

You will learn how to use layman's terms for complex medical or industry language and how to provide an analogy that any listener can relate to immediately.

You will learn how to focus your eyes, how to use gestures and body language in a confident and animated manner. You will learn pivotal skills in calming the mind and reducing anxiety ahead of an interview. In addition, you will learn how to stop the common UMMS and AHHS and pause instead.

Book your media training workshop by emailing: info@greenlightpr.com.au
or visit www.greenlightpr.com.au

ABOUT THE AUTHOR

AMANDA MILLS

Amanda Mills has worked as a senior publicist in Australia for 20 years specialising in the health, retail, education, hospitality and tourism sectors. Amanda provides media training to business owners, medical experts and health and wellness professionals, helping them deliver interviews with confidence and clarity.

www.ingramcontent.com/pod-product-compliance
Lightning Source LLC
Chambersburg PA
CBHW072132070526
44585CB00016B/1641